GROWING TOGETHER IN

COURAGE

GROWING TOGETHER IN

COURAGE

CHARACTER STORIES FOR **FAMILIES**

FAMILYLIFE®

Little Rock, Arkansas

BARBARA RAINEY

GROWING TOGETHER IN COURAGE

FamilyLife Publishing®
5800 Ranch Drive
Little Rock, Arkansas 72223
1-800-FL-TODAY • FamilyLife.com
FLTI, d/b/a FamilyLife®, is a ministry of Campus Crusade for Christ International®

Unless otherwise noted, Scripture quotations are from the New American Standard Bible®, Copyright © The Lockman Foundation 1960, 1962, 1963, 1968, 1971, 1972, 1973, 1975, 1977, 1995. Used by permission. (www.Lockman.org)

Scripture quotations marked (ESV) are taken from the Holy Bible, English Standard Version, copyright © 2001 by Crossway Bibles, a division of Good News Publishers. Used by permission. All rights reserved.

Scripture quotations marked (KJV) are taken from the King James Version of the Bible.

The prayers in the "Praying Together for Courage" sections of each chapter have been adapted from Arthur G. Bennett, ed., *The Valley of Vision: A Collection of Puritan Prayers and Devotions* (Carlisle, PA: Banner of Truth, 2002), 204, 23, 19, 191, 33, 185 (respectively).

ISBN: 978-1-60200-358-3

Design: Brand Navigation, LLC

Printed in the United States of America
2010—First Edition

14 13 12 11 10   1 2 3 4 5

FAMILYLIFE®
Help for today. Hope for tomorrow.

dedicated to

James Escue

A heart of compassion is yours,

Given by the Good Shepherd

That you may be mighty for his kingdom.

Be courageous.

Be an overcomer.

For he calls you and all his children to step into the fray

To cooperate with the King of Heaven

By being his hands and feet of love.

May you show others

The victories of courageous faith

All the days of your life.

CONTENTS

WHY TALK ABOUT

Joshua was afraid. His best friend and mentor had just died, and now God was giving him the biggest assignment of his life. Joshua was to lead the nation of God's people into their new land of promise. They would face many enemies and fight many battles before the land became their home.

Joshua needed courage, so God said to him, "Have I not commanded you? Be strong and courageous. Do not be frightened, and do not be dismayed, for the LORD your God is with you wherever you go" (Joshua 1:9, ESV).

Courage may be easy to define, but it usually comes into our lives through hard choices. When facing an unpredictable situation, the decision must be made: to do the right thing or the easy thing, to sacrifice for others or be selfish, to act in faith or give in to our feelings. As it was with Joshua, so it is with us: The difference between courage and cowardice is found not in our own strength but in God's, and in our ability to trust him. It's a decision of belief: Will we do what the Bible teaches, or will we go our own way? Will we find our security in God's promise to always be with us, or will we look for security in other places?

Families need to talk about courage because we and our children will all have moments of difficulty that demand hard decisions of faith. Our children need to see us confront fearful situations with courage so that they will be inspired to exhibit courage in the midst of their own fears. Dan Hayes, director of Community Ministries in Atlanta, says, "Courage is not the absence of fear . . . [it] is the ability to do that which you do fear." As parents, we need to teach our children not to let fear overwhelm them, but instead to remember that God promised to never leave them or forsake them. We also

COURAGE?

need to encourage our children to move into every challenge and crisis, bravely believing in God's presence.

Every year during the Easter season, we think of Jesus' obedience to the Father's will, his love for us, and his suffering. Because of his choices, we call Jesus surrendered, loving, and sacrificial; but have you ever heard him called courageous? He was! I believe that Jesus the man was more courageous than anyone who ever lived, because he acted not for his own benefit but for ours, and only to please the Father. He was never selfish; he was always selfless. Jesus is the supreme example of courage. He made the ultimate sacrifice—giving his life—to save all who choose to believe.

The stories in this small book are intended to inspire courage, to call each one in your family to live for the Savior. May we all be found bravely following him, knowing that just as God was with Joshua—"for the LORD your God is with you wherever you go"—so he will be with us.

Barbara Rainey

COURAGE

MEMORY VERSE

"Have I not commanded you? Be strong and courageous. Do not be frightened, and do not be dismayed, for the LORD your God is with you wherever you go." —JOSHUA 1:9, ESV

the white rose
courage speaks the truth

SOPHIE
SCHOLL
† 22. II.
1943

DEUTSCHE BUNDESPOST

20

Would you ever risk your own safety to protect a friend? Would you be brave enough to speak the truth if you knew the consequences might bring you harm? Or harder still, would you risk your life for a person you didn't even know?

Meet Sophie Scholl, who answered yes to all of these questions.

Sophie grew up in Germany in the 1920s and '30s, the fourth of six children. Her parents worked to provide a nurturing family environment that included a thorough education both at school and at church. Yet even with such a safe life at home, the world around Sophie and her family was changing rapidly and becoming dangerous.

In 1933, Adolph Hitler became the leader of Germany. Because he believed that certain people were superior and that others weren't fit to be free or even to live, Hitler used his army to intimidate and arrest millions of people. Some he put in prison; others he gave orders to execute. People lived in constant terror. Some were so frightened that they moved out of their homes and

> Let no one look down on your youthfulness.
>
> —1 TIMOTHY 4:12

> **Would you risk your life for a person you didn't even know?**

began living in the woods and in caves—anywhere they thought they could hide from Hitler's army.

When she was sixteen, Sophie watched as her older brother, Hans, was arrested with a group of friends for expressing ideas that opposed the Third Reich,* the name given to Hitler's governmental regime. Then one of her favorite teachers from high school was taken suddenly from the classroom, beaten in the street by soldiers, and loaded onto a train with thousands of other Jews, never to return. Following her high-school graduation, Sophie was required to join the auxiliary war service, where she learned about the "Final Solution," Hitler's plan to exterminate the Jewish population of Europe. All of these events left Sophie troubled. She was intensely saddened and outraged. She prayed and studied her Bible more than ever, trying to find answers, desperate for hope and direction.

---

*See Reference Points on page 33 for descriptions of certain terms, titles, and historical figures.

While attending the University of Munich in 1942, Sophie and Hans began talking about what they could do. They felt so inadequate. After all, they were just students. But how could they close their eyes to the evil around them? Injustices were everywhere.

Together with a group of friends, Hans and Sophie decided to write and distribute pamphlets that would tell the truth about the atrocities being committed by the German authorities. They named themselves the White Rose, a symbol of purity and innocence. For Sophie, the White Rose represented the purity of God's truth, which she felt must be defended against the evil that the Third Reich was perpetrating against the Jews. Soon the White Rose became an underground movement dedicated to inspiring the German people to rise up and overthrow Hitler and his regime.

Early one February morning in 1943, members of the White Rose were distributing pamphlets in the empty halls of the university. A janitor saw Sophie toss the last of her bundle over a balcony and called the Gestapo, the German secret police. Within the hour, Sophie, Hans, and a friend, Christoph Probst, were arrested.

Even under intense questioning and pressure, Sophie never broke. Speaking boldly to her prison guards and cell mates, she said, "Should we stand here at the end of the war with empty hands when they ask the question, 'What did you do?' and we must answer, 'Nothing'?"[1]

A Nazi judge pronounced the three young activists guilty of treason. When brought before the judge for sentencing, Sophie said, "I still believe that I acted in the best interests of my people. I would do it again. I will accept the consequences."[2] Just three days later, Sophie, Hans, and Christoph were beheaded. Sophie was only twenty-one.

The following summer, one of the pamphlets Sophie had died to deliver was smuggled out of Germany, reprinted by the millions in England, and dropped by plane all over Germany. After reading the words of truth that fluttered like snow from the sky, once frightened men and women became emboldened to join the resistance movement, just as Sophie and Hans had dreamed of.

Sophie and the members of the White Rose courageously lived out their faith, refusing to be silent and safe when the lives of millions were at risk. Courageous faith is like that—determined, strong, and brave in the face of potential suffering, grounded in the knowledge that pleasing God by speaking the truth is more important than personal safety.

Learn more about the life of Sophie Scholl by watching the movie *Sophie Scholl: The Final Days*, DVD, directed by Marc Rothemund (New York: Zeitgeist Films, 2005).

questions about courage

Courageous faith may not send you to your death, but taking a stand for what is right and true could invite rejection from others.

- What might have happened if others had stood up against Hitler's evil before he became so powerful?
- Have you ever believed something so strongly, like Sophie and Hans did, that it came with a cost? What did it cost you?
- What cause, if any, do you believe God wants you to stand up for? Who needs to hear the truth about Jesus from you?

The scripture at the beginning of this story—"Let no one look down on your youthfulness"—reminds us that God isn't hindered by our age. Just as he used Sophie and the White Rose, he is looking for other young people who are willing to be courageous for the truth.

recognizing courage

If there were such a thing as the "Sophie Scholl Award," given to a person for courageously trying to protect either a friend or a stranger, who would you nominate to receive the reward?

I would nominate _____ because _____

_____

praying together for courage

Heavenly Father, you are good when you give and when you take away. You are good when the sun shines on us and when the dark of night hovers over us. Help us in sunshine and shadow to remember that you never change. And may we be strengthened to speak the truth courageously that our words may be used to push back the darkness of our day. (Adapted from *The Valley of Vision*.)

a lion meets the lionhearted

courage says no to self

Lions are powerful, able to kill with speed and strength. The lion has no natural predators; he is king. All other animals fear his power.

For much of his life, Denver Moore was known as a lion. Born in poverty in Red River Parish, Louisiana, Denver never went to school. He didn't know that there was any other kind of life than picking cotton for "the Man," the plantation owner.

"All them years," Denver said, "there was a freight train that used to roll through Red River Parish. Ever day, I'd hear it whistle and moan and I used to imagine it callin out about the places it could take me. One day I got tired a' bein poor. So I walked out to the highway, waited for that train to slow down some, and jumped on it. I didn't get off till the doors opened up again in Ft. Worth, Texas."[1]

Denver was twenty-seven years old, and he soon decided that Fort Worth was a decent place to live. "When a black man who can't read, can't write, can't figger, and don't know how to work

> Do not merely look out for your own personal interests, but also for the interests of others.
> —PHILIPPIANS 2:4

> "I'm a bad man and you better not mess with me."

nothin but cotton comes to the big city, he don't have too many of what white folks call 'career opportunities.'"[2]

Over time he learned that people would sometimes hand him a dollar or two and that work crews would occasionally hire homeless men for twenty dollars a day. It was a rough life, but he reasoned that it was better than being a slave on a plantation.

Denver lived like this for more than twenty years. People on the streets called him a lion because he was mean and dangerous—always on guard against anyone who would invade his space.

Then something happened to Denver that changed his life. His experience was much like the story in the Bible about a man who was robbed and beaten and left to die by the side of the road. Two religious leaders walked by the injured man but did nothing to help him. Then another man, a Samaritan, came by. Unlike the others, he stopped to help, taking the injured man to an inn where he could be cared for.

Denver Moore was like that injured man. He had fallen to the side of the road as a teenager,

7

and for years no one took the time to care for him. Until Miss Debbie came along.

Debbie and her husband, Ron, lived a comfortable life in Fort Worth, but Debbie volunteered at the Union Gospel Mission. One day she spotted Denver, and her heart broke for him. A greater contradiction cannot be imagined: He was a huge black man; she a petite white woman. He lived on the streets; she in a mansion. He never owned more than the clothes on his back; she had an abundance he could never have dreamed of.

Tough and withdrawn, Denver would often come to eat at the mission. He refused to talk, but Debbie was persistent. One day she asked him his name, and he responded in an angry voice, "You don't need to know my name. I'm a bad man and you better not mess with me."[3]

Debbie jumped around the counter, got right in his face, and said, "You are not a bad man, you are a good man. God has a calling on your life and you are going to live to see it!"[4]

Debbie pursued Denver. She never gave up.

"I ain't gon' sugarcoat it: The streets'll turn a man nasty," recalls Denver. "And I had been nasty, homeless, in scrapes with the law, in Angola prison, and homeless again for a lotta years by the time I met Miss Debbie. I want to tell you this about her: She was the skinniest, noisiest, pushiest woman I had ever met, black or white. For a long time I tried to stay outta her way. But after a while, Miss Debbie got me to talkin 'bout things I don't like to talk about and tellin things I ain't never told nobody."[5]

Courage doesn't pause to think, *What will happen to me if I help this man?* Instead, Debbie thought, *What will happen to him if I don't?* Over time, Denver displayed courage too as he slowly set aside his fear, opened up to her, and chose to trust—something people who live on the streets seldom do. He dropped his self-protection enough to let someone love him.

Eight years after Miss Debbie told Denver that God had a plan for his life, he stood in the ballroom of a grand hotel to receive an award for his work on behalf of the homeless. He had learned to read and write and was by then serving on the board of the Union Gospel Mission. He had also begun to travel and speak in various cities, helping to raise money for rescue missions throughout the United States.

Denver's life had been changed because one woman—one little woman—didn't think about her own interests but had the courage to see a need and do something about it.

Read Denver Moore's inspiring story in the book *Same Kind of Different as Me* (Nashville: Thomas Nelson, 2006) by Ron Hall and Denver Moore.

questions about courage

Courage not only helps us see a person in need, but it also motivates us to reach out and do something.

- What might have happened if the Good Samaritan had thought about how much money it was going to cost him to help the man on the side of the road, or how bloody and dirty his clothes would get when he picked up the man to put him on his donkey?
- Are you willing to risk others snickering at you if you spend time reaching out to someone who isn't popular or lovely?
- Think of someone in your neighborhood or school who needs to be cared for and shown God's love. What could you do to demonstrate God's love to them?

At the beginning of this story, we read, "Do not merely look out for your own personal interests, but also for the interests of others." This scripture is followed two verses later by the example of Jesus, who "made himself nothing, taking the form of a servant" (Philippians 2:7, ESV). Jesus always said no to self, which is why he is our ultimate example of courage, the One we should follow.

recognizing courage

Miss Debbie met Denver while she was serving food at a rescue mission in her hometown. Where are some places you could go in your community to help people who are less fortunate than you? What could you do for them?

I could go to _____ and help people there by _____

praying together for courage

Father, as the all-seeing One, nothing escapes your notice. But we walk past the needs of others every day. Help us to redeem the time, to be awake to the love and care you have for your children. May we feed the hungry, clothe the naked, teach the illiterate, forgive the offender, and show neighborly love to all. Through our actions may others see Jesus in us. (Adapted from *The Valley of Vision*.)

a tale of two mothers
courage refuses fear

Have you ever watched a class of preschoolers walking to the playground? The children hold on to a rope so that none of them will get separated from the group; then they follow their teacher as she leads them outside. They move together in a line, each child following the person in front.

Through the centuries, millions of Christians have gone before us. They are faith ancestors, people from previous generations whose lives still influence us today. And we, like a group of children, are holding on to the rope of faith, following those ahead of us and learning from their words and actions. For more than two thousand years, this procession has steadily moved forward. So many have gone before us that we can't possibly count them all. We know the names of but a few, and yet someday in heaven, we will know them all.

Today let's meet two women and hear their stories of courageous faith. Then when you meet them one day, you'll say, "Oh, I know part of your story. Tell me more!"

Catharine duBois lived in the 1600s in what is now the state of New York. In the midst of a

> Fear not for I am with you; be not dismayed, for I am your God; I will strengthen you, I will help you, I will uphold you with my righteous right hand. —ISAIAH 41:10, ESV

> *"Have you given your child unreservedly to the Lord for whatever he wills?"*

terrifying event, she responded with such courageous faith that her story still inspires her family eight generations later. One of her descendants, who became a magazine editor, wrote this about Catharine:

> One day in 1663, Minisink Indians swept down from the Catskill Mountains, killed several inhabitants of the little settlement now known as New Paltz, New York, and took a number of women and children captive. Among them were Catharine duBois and her infant daughter, Sara. For ten weeks they were held captive in the mountains while search parties looked for them in vain.
>
> Certain they had avoided reprisal, the Indians decided to celebrate their success by burning Catharine and Sara. A pile of logs was arranged, upon which the bound mother and daughter were placed.
>
> A most human response at this moment would have been for Catharine to scream at her

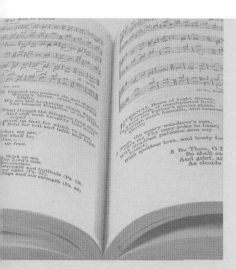

tormentors, curse them for her suffering, or even curse God. Instead, she burst into song, turning the foreboding Catskill forest into a cathedral of praise.

The Minisink Indians, of course, had not asked her for a song, but they were now so captivated with Catharine's singing that they demanded another song, then another, and then still another. And while she sang, her husband, Louis, and his search party burst upon the scene and rescued her.

Catharine could not have known that her decision about how to die would tell her succeeding generations much about how they should live. Nor can we know how some decision today will affect generations to come.[1]

Two hundred years later, there lived another Catherine—Catherine Carmichael—whose daughter Amy desired to become a missionary in India. When Amy, at the age of twenty-four, wrote her mother to ask if she had "given her child unreservedly to the Lord" to do his will, Catherine wrote in reply:

My own precious child; yes, dearest Amy, He has lent you to me all these years. He only knows what a strength, comfort and joy you have been to me. So, darling, when He asks you now to go away from within my reach, can I say no? No, Amy, He is yours—you are His—to take you where He pleases and to use you as He pleases.[2]

Catherine Carmichael could have been afraid that Amy would never return home from India, or she might have feared that some great tragedy would befall her. But Catherine rejected such fear. She, like Catharine duBois, voiced faith in God's great love and plan, which they both believed were superior to their own wishes. They believed God's promise: "Fear not for I am with you; be not dismayed, for I am your God; I will strengthen you, I will help you" (Isaiah 41:10, ESV). The protection of their own lives and the lives of their children was best left in God's hands.

When any difficult choice is before us, fear will whisper—or even shout—the what-ifs in our hearts. But God knows how easy it is for us to fear, and so he promised to be with us always. His presence gives us courage.

Read more about the life of Amy Carmichael in Elisabeth Elliot's book *A Chance to Die: The Life and Legacy of Amy Carmichael* (Grand Rapids: Revell, 2005).

questions about courage

Are you ever afraid? Recognizing fear and naming its source are essential in overcoming fear and becoming courageous.

- What fears are keeping you from courageous faith?
- Can faith and fear coexist? Why or why not?
- How does knowing that God will never leave you or forsake you help you be brave?
- A Welsh preacher named Martyn Lloyd-Jones once said, "Faith is the refusal to panic." How did the two women exhibit a refusal to panic or to give in to their fears? How can you?

Remembering that God is always with you will help you fight your fears (Isaiah 41:10).

recognizing courage

Can you think of a "faith ancestor" you would like to meet someday—a Christian who lived in an earlier time whose life still influences you and your family? Who is this person, and what would you like to discuss with him or her?

I look forward to meeting _____ I want to ask him or her about _____

praying together for courage

Father, the One who hears his children, what a wonder it is to know that your Son, Jesus, is always before you representing all who call upon you in his name. As he represents us in heaven, may we bravely reflect him on earth, and while he pleads our cause, may we give him praise in every situation, especially when we are most afraid, for in that moment of faith we will be strengthened. (Adapted from *The Valley of Vision*.)

three hurdles to the finish line

courage overcomes obstacles

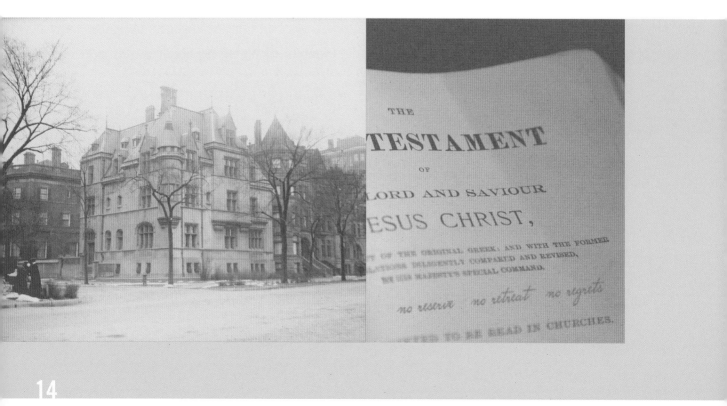

Do you know what hurdles are? In the sport of track and field, there's a race called the four-hundred-meter hurdles. You not only run in this race, but you must also jump over "hurdles" that look like small fences. You can't run around them; you have to jump over them. It isn't an easy race; it requires courage, stamina, and a great deal of training.

Life is like running in a four-hundred-meter hurdle race. In order to do what God wants us to do, we have to get past the obstacles that get in our way. Many have overcome great obstacles in their lives—people like Jackie Robinson, Martin Luther King Jr., and Helen Keller, to name a few. And then there's William Borden.

William was born in Chicago in 1887 into a family of great wealth. William's mother was a devoted follower of Christ, and at age seven, little William surrendered his life to Christ as well. He never departed from that childhood decision of faith.

When William graduated from high school at age sixteen, he was already a millionaire. As a

> Let us run with endurance the race that is set before us.
>
> —HEBREWS 12:1

> *"A life abandoned to Christ cannot be cut short."*

graduation gift, his father arranged for William to travel around the world so that he might experience other cultures firsthand.

On the ship William met missionaries who were on their way to China, Japan, and Korea, and he was impressed by their sacrifice. While in India, William resolved to leave his life of ease behind to serve others. He wrote to his mother, "I have so much of everything in this life, and there are so many millions who have nothing and live in darkness."[1]

One of his friends back in Chicago was shocked by William's desire and wrote a letter imploring him not to "throw yourself away as a missionary."[2] In response to the letter, William wrote in his Bible these two words: "No reserve."[3]

After returning home, William entered Yale University, hoping to distinguish himself by his love for Jesus rather than his wealth. As a freshman, he chose friends who were also interested in spiritual truth. He began a prayer and Bible-study group, which by the end of the year, had grown to 150 students. William also worked with the homeless in the university town of New Haven,

Connecticut. He began the Yale Hope Mission to reach those who had no hope, and he was often seen on his knees praying with drunken men and encouraging them to go to the mission for help.

William rejected the party lifestyle of a college student, refusing to waste his time and money on entertainment and pleasure. Instead, he chose this verse as the goal for his college years: "Thy word have I hid in mine heart, that I might not sin against thee" (Psalm 119:11, KJV).

When William graduated from college, he was offered many high-paying jobs, but he refused them all. His desire was set, and his goal was clear—he had decided to go to China to reach the Muslim Kansu people with the gospel. In his Bible he wrote two more words: "No retreat."[4]

One more step was necessary for William: graduate study at Princeton Seminary. Like his college experience, William's seminary days were marked by active involvement in the lives of others. He taught a Sunday-school class at an African Episcopal church and gave away thousands of dollars to Christian ministries.

After completing his seminary courses, William set sail for Egypt, where he planned to study the Muslim culture and religion before going on to China. Tragically, from our perspective, just a few short months after arriving in Egypt, he contracted spinal meningitis and died at the age of twenty-five. The news was carried across America in most every newspaper. It was written of him, "Borden not only gave away his wealth, but himself, in a way so joyous and natural that it seemed a privilege rather than a sacrifice."[5] One of his good friends said after hearing the news, "I have absolutely no feeling of a life cut short. A life abandoned to Christ cannot be cut short."[6]

When his mother received William's personal belongings, she found his Bible among them. In it he had written two more words: "No regrets."[7]

Three hurdles stood in William's path—the opinion of his friends, the snare of prosperity, and the fear of being abandoned by God—and William overcame each one. As he lay dying in Egypt far from home, he could easily have felt that God had forgotten about him. But his words "no regrets" tell us that even in his darkest hour, William's faith overcame all fear. He was strong and courageous to the end, assured of the promise, "The LORD your God is with you wherever you go" (Joshua 1:9).

William's life is still speaking to us. The words he wrote in his Bible call us to overcome our obstacles and live courageously for Christ, just as William did.

Learn more about the life of William Borden in Mrs. Howard Taylor's book *Borden of Yale* (Minneapolis: Bethany House, 1988).

questions about courage

God often uses obstacles to build our faith. Each of us can become more courageous as we learn to face and overcome our individual challenges.

- What are the obstacles in the race of your life right now?
- Are your friendships a hurdle or a stumbling block in your life? If so, in what way?
- How has prosperity or the desire to live the good life been a hindrance to you?
- Are you living a life of courage for that which will last? Explain.

Remember, God will give the strength you need to run your race and overcome every obstacle. "Run with endurance." (Hebrews 12:1). Don't quit!

recognizing courage

The words William Borden wrote in his Bible—"No reserve. No retreat. No regrets."—summarized how he wanted to live his life for God's purposes. What words describe how you want to live?

No _____   No _____   No _____

praying together for courage

All-wise God, your never-failing providence orders every event, all our comings and goings. You have great purposes for your children's lives, good works that you have created us to do, designed specifically for each one. Help us not to miss that for which we were made. Keep us from being distracted by the lesser loyalties of money and prestige and power. May our goal be to follow the path you have for us individually that we may have no regrets at the finish line of life. (Adapted from *The Valley of Vision*.)

today matters forever

courage is countercultural

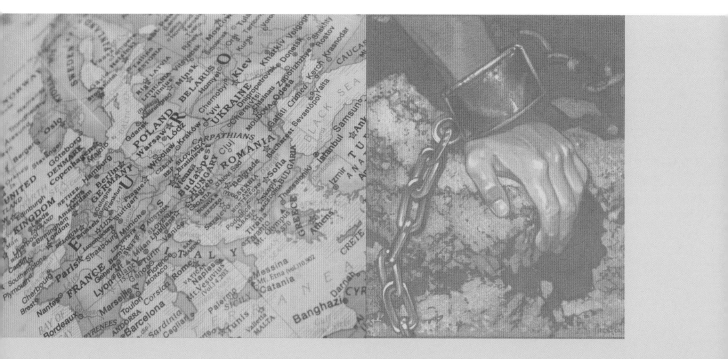

Have you ever been canoeing? Paddling downstream takes very little effort; the water just moves you along. But what is it like to paddle a canoe upstream? It takes a lot more work, because going against the current, or flow, requires strength and determination.

To be *countercultural* means to go against the flow. It means doing what is right and true no matter what others are doing. When you go against the flow, you recognize that just because something is popular doesn't necessarily mean that it's right.

Courage is countercultural.

In 1945, an assembly of pastors and priests gathered in Bucharest, Romania. The meeting had been organized by the new Soviet-controlled Communist government, which had recently replaced Hitler's Nazi government in Romania. Neither government allowed true freedom of religion. The Romanian people had suffered under Hitler and were about to suffer under a new, equally cruel leader, Joseph Stalin.

Do not be anxious about how you should defend yourself.

—LUKE 12:11, ESV

"I do not wish to have a coward for a husband."

Richard Wurmbrand and his wife, Sabina, were at the 1945 gathering. They knew that a primary intent of Communism was to destroy religion, so they were shocked to hear many of their fellow religious leaders actually declaring a belief that Communism and Christianity could peacefully coexist. Because of fear, these men set aside their faith and spoke with lies and flattery.

Deeply troubled, Sabina whispered to her husband, "Richard, stand up and wash away this shame from the face of Christ."

"If I speak," Richard explained, "you will lose your husband."

Sabina replied, "I do not wish to have a coward for a husband."[1]

Sabina displayed extraordinary courage in this bold challenge to her husband. She knew she could lose him to prison or even death for speaking out against the Communist government. But she wasn't thinking of her own security. What was right and true was more important to her than personal comfort.

While the other church leaders were more interested in pleasing men than God, Richard left no doubt as to where his allegiances lay. Making his way to the stage, and to everyone's surprise, he began to preach:

"Delegates, it is our duty not to praise earthly powers that come and go, but to glorify God the Creator and Christ the Savior, who died for us on the cross."

A Communist official jumped to his feet. This would not do! The whole country was hearing the message of Christ proclaimed from the rostrum of the Communist Parliament. "Your right to speak is withdrawn!" he shouted.

Wurmbrand ignored him and went on. The atmosphere began to change. The audience began to applaud. He was saying what they had all wanted to say, but were afraid to.[2]

After this, Richard Wurmbrand was a marked man. On Sunday, February 29, 1948, while on his way to church, Wurmbrand was taken captive by the secret police and taken to a prison thirty feet beneath the earth's surface. There he was placed in solitary confinement. For years he had no other human contact than with the guards who interrogated and beat him. Still, Richard knew that God had not forgotten him.

After eight and a half years, Richard Wurmbrand was released in 1956. Sabina had been in prison for three of those years herself, forced into hard labor and subjected to countless interrogations.

Because Richard continued to share the gospel and speak the truth after his release, he was arrested again and imprisoned for an additional five years! Finally, a ransom was paid to the Romanian government for his freedom, and this time he and Sabina left the country. In England and then later in the United States, they continued their work to reach Communists with the gospel and to help others who were being persecuted for their faith.

Richard and Sabina Wurmbrand paid a much higher price for their courage than you may be asked to pay. Still, there will be times in your life when you will need to be countercultural—to go against the flow—and show more concern for doing what is right than doing what is popular.

Learn more about the persecuted church around the world by visiting the Voice of the Martyrs Web site Persecution.com.

questions about courage

Even if we stand alone, our courage will probably help others in ways we may never know. Courage is never unnoticed.

- Perhaps your friends are all going to a certain movie, but you aren't sure you should go, or your parents have said no. Do you go anyway to fit in with your friends, or are you willing to stand alone?
- Your family may be struggling financially. Do you stop tithing to save money, or do you continue to give as the Bible teaches, trusting God to honor your faith?
- Why is it important to do right even if it is a difficult and perhaps unpopular thing to do?

Remember that God will give you the courage to do what is right no matter how many are against you or how few are with you. He promises to teach you "in that very hour" (Luke 12:11–12).

recognizing courage

Can you think of others who, like the Wurmbrands, have shown faith and courage by doing what was right even though it wasn't popular? List the names of people whose courage you remember.

_____   _____   _____

_____   _____   _____

praying together for courage

Our Redeemer, the price you paid for our rescue is beyond comprehension. Yet our small understanding helps us know we can never repay the cost. So our task is to make you and your limitless love known to others. Help us to be strong and courageous in speaking for you when all is against us. May we never be swayed by popular opinion but stay close to your side, listening to your voice, following your footsteps, no matter the cost.

to ethiopia with love
courage is active

Have you ever watched someone being courageous? Perhaps you've seen a student at your school help break up a fight, or a motorist stop to help someone who's been in a wreck. You might even remember the terrorist attacks on September 11, 2001. Even though it was a terrifying day in our nation, there were heroes among us. We called them "first responders"—police officers, firefighters, and medics who ran toward the danger to help those who were wounded and afraid. Their bravery brought hope to us all.

We admire those who see a need and then do something about it in spite of the risks to their own lives. The person who stands on the shore and hopes that a drowning man will be saved doesn't impress us. But we'll never forget the one who jumps into the water, swims to the drowning man, and pulls him safely to shore.

To be courageous, we must be willing to leave our place of comfort and safety to help people in need. That's what Paul and Susan Lim did.

For the love of Christ controls us.
—2 CORINTHIANS 5:14

"Christ does not call us to a prudent life, but to a . . . life of love and courage."

The Lims are both medical doctors—he a plastic surgeon, and she a pediatrician. A few years ago they made the brave decision to leave the comfort of their home in Minneapolis and move to the country of Ethiopia, where the number of children in need of medical care far outnumbers the doctors available to give it. Even though many of their friends challenged their decision at the time—arguing that the Lims could support missionaries by staying in Minnesota and making hundreds of thousands of dollars—Paul and Susan knew that someone must be willing to go.

Something their pastor said helped them reach this decision: "Christ does not call us to a prudent life, but to a God-centered, Christ-exalting, justice-advancing, counter-cultural, risk-taking life of love and courage."[1]

Life isn't nearly so easy or comfortable for the Lims in Ethiopia as it was at home. They've had to stand in long lines at government agencies to get the proper paperwork for building a hospital and repairing their home. Every task is much more difficult than it was in the United States, but they persevered in the construction of a sixty-bed hospital, where Paul can now perform surgery

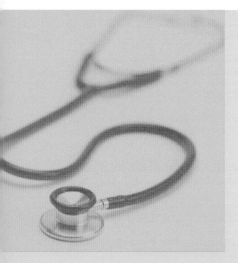

and Susan can provide aftercare. They've been willing to endure the hardships because they know they are doing what God has called them to do.

But the Lims offer so much more than medical care to their patients. Among the many children they've treated is ten-year-old Mohammed, whose father gave him this name so that he would be Allah's servant. When he was a baby, Mohammed fell into a fire and was burned severely. Their village was in a very remote location, and the parents walked two days to get help for him, but there was very little that could be done. When they returned home, the father felt that they had been cursed for this to have happened, so he told his wife to throw little Mohammed away so the lions or hyenas would kill him. But she refused.

For seven years this little boy lived in constant pain from burn wounds that wouldn't heal. One day his mother heard about the Lims' hospital in Addis Ababa and decided to make the long journey there. Shortly after she and Mohammed arrived at the hospital, Dr. Paul and another doctor began treatments and surgeries on the young boy. Through the care Mohammed and his mother received at the hospital, she gave her life to Jesus. The love of the staff and workers drew her in, and she understood the good news of the gospel.

Hundreds of children and family members have been greeted at the hospital with the love, warmth, and compassion of Jesus. The Lims' courageous faith to serve these people is something that Jesus calls all his followers to do. Just as he sent out his disciples, Jesus sends believers out into the world today too. Faith is active.

In an e-mail update to friends, Dr. Lim wrote, "Ethiopia is a crossroad of Christian and Muslim influence. As I see many in this region in great peril both in this life and in the life to come, I'm glad to be here to do something about it and wait with eager anticipation to see how the Lord works here through your prayers."[2]

Paul and Susan are making a great difference in many lives, but the need is still immense, and the task is far greater than they can accomplish alone. The call of God for each man, woman, boy, and girl is to be his arms of love, his hands of healing, his voice of encouragement and hope to those in need who surround us.

Where does God want you to begin?

For more information about the Lims and the organization they work with—CURE International—visit the Web site CureInternational.org.

questions about courage

It's not just adults who can serve those in need. Children have had some wonderful ideas for helping the homeless in their towns and cities, helping orphans and foster children, or raising money to help those in need in other countries.

- Why don't you take some time to talk with your family and dream about what you can do? What action can your family take to help someone in need?
- Are you willing to go where God calls you? There is no greater joy than cooperating with him in an adventure of courageous faith.

Remember, courage is active. May we be motivated by the love of Christ to serve others (2 Corinthians 5:14).

recognizing courage

There are approximately 195 nations in our world, each one needing the prayers and compassion of God's people. Can you think of a country you would like to pray for—perhaps a country where a friend, family member, or missionary you've met is living? Pray for that country each day for the following week.

I will pray for the country of   I will pray that

praying together for courage

Sustainer of Life, we know that you have numbered our days. Whether they be many or few, help us to remember that there can be no true happiness, no fulfilling purpose of life apart from a life lived in and for your Son, Jesus. Help us overcome all that stands in our path to knowing his love, which is worthy of all sacrifice. (Adapted from *The Valley of Vision*.)

miracles in a blue volkswagen

courage takes risks

Have you ever seen a miracle?

A miracle happens when God does something that we humans cannot do. The Bible tells many stories of miraculous events that took place long ago. Remember Joshua and the walls of Jericho, Moses parting the Red Sea, or Jesus feeding more than five thousand people with just five loaves of bread and two fish?

Do you think that miracles still happen today, or were they only for Bible times? Before you answer, you might want to know something about Brother Andrew.

Some people called him "God's smuggler" because Brother Andrew would often sneak Bibles into Communist countries, where having a Bible was illegal. If he had been caught, he would have been thrown in prison, but God honored Brother Andrew's courage, sometimes even performing miracles to protect him.

One day, as Brother Andrew was waiting in his little blue Volkswagen to cross the border into

> "Behold, I am the LORD, the God of all flesh; is anything too difficult for Me?"
> —JEREMIAH 32:27

> "Dare I ask for a miracle?"

Yugoslavia, he started thinking about the great risk he was taking. The armed guards at the border were searching the cars and luggage and making sure that each person had the proper paperwork to allow them into the country. Brother Andrew knew that his paperwork was in order, but he also knew that his car was loaded with Bibles and other Christian literature. If the guards found any of this, he would be arrested and taken to prison. But Brother Andrew knew something else: The Christian believers in Yugoslavia were suffering and in desperate need of the encouragement that the literature he was smuggling into the country would bring them. He had to try, even if it meant prison.

So that day he prayed a prayer that was to be repeated hundreds of times in the years to come:

Lord, in my luggage I have Scripture that I want to take to Your children across this border. When You were on earth, You made blind eyes see. Now, I pray, make seeing eyes blind. Do not let the guards see those things You do not want them to see.[1]

Finally Brother Andrew's turn came. The guards took his paperwork and began poking around in the car. One guard asked to see inside his suitcase, which was filled with Christian tracts. As Brother Andrew opened it, there in plain sight were the tracts. The guard asked, "Do you have anything else to declare?"

Andrew replied, "Only small things."

"We won't bother with them," said the guard as he handed back the paperwork and waved Andrew on.[2]

God had made seeing eyes blind!

Several years later, on a trip to Romania, Brother Andrew again saw the power of God at work. As he pulled up to the border crossing in his Volkswagen, he saw only six cars ahead of him and concluded that it would be a short wait. But he was soon proved wrong as the first car in line sat still for thirty minutes before being allowed to move on. The next car was emptied of its passengers, who were then instructed to unpack every item in the car. Forty minutes later, they reloaded the car and drove through the checkpoint. For the next car, the guards removed the hubcaps and seats and then took the engine apart.

Recalling what happened next, Andrew wrote,

It was my turn. I put the little VW in gear, inched my way forward, handed the guard my papers, and started to get out. But his knee was against the door, holding it closed. He looked at my photograph, scribbled something down, shoved the papers back to me and abruptly waved me on.

Not thirty seconds had passed. I started the engine and inched forward. Was I supposed to pull over? Was I . . . surely I wasn't . . . I coasted forward, my foot poised above the brake. Nothing happened. I looked in my rearview mirror. The guard was motioning the next driver out of his car and pointing for him to open the hood.

My heart was racing. Not with the excitement of the crossing, but with the excitement of having caught such a spectacular glimpse of God at work.[5]

Would God do that for you? He might if you give him your life and go where he calls you to go. Every day there are opportunities to put courage in action and trust God to work through you—in your school, your office, your neighborhood.

Read more about Brother Andrew's life in the book *God's Smuggler* (Grand Rapids: Chosen Books, 2001).

questions about courage

There are still many countries in our world where it's dangerous to be known as a Christian, where having a Bible and teaching from it could invite harassment and persecution.

- Can you name some of the places in our world that are dangerous for Christians? How can you pray for the people in these places?
- Talk about other ways you and your family might help these brothers and sisters in Christ. Are you willing to be a Brother Andrew in this generation?
- There are also many believers who just need to be encouraged in their faith. Some may live in your community. What can you do for them so they will not lose hope in believing?

Remember, courage takes risks; it recognizes that bravery comes from God. Nothing is too difficult for him (Jeremiah 32:27).

recognizing courage

When we give ourselves to live for eternal purposes, as Brother Andrew did, God sometimes demonstrates his power in unexpected ways. What other stories have you heard about God performing miracles and doing unexpected things? List them here:

praying together for courage

You are a miracle-working Father, and to belong to you is a gift beyond measure. To see you work miracles in our hard and stubborn hearts is as wondrous as watching you make seeing eyes blind. Help us to so align our lives with your purposes that we too might experience the privilege of watching the Almighty at work. May we then tell the stories of your power on display that others may want to follow you and so enter eternity with us on that day!

RECOGNIZING COURAGE

date

Keep looking for displays of courage. When your faith is strengthened by the courage that you see in others, record it below and share it with your family. Be sure to applaud courage in your family. May each of you become known as a courageous Christian.

date

REFERENCE POINTS

DAY ONE: **The Third Reich** means "the third empire or rule." Hitler's forces called themselves this to make it sound as if they were the third great empire in Germany's history.

DAY TWO: **The plantation owner** that Denver Moore worked for ran a sharecropping system of farming. This was often the way large farms were operated in the southern United States after the Civil War. The landowner let other farmers rent his land in exchange for a share of the crop.

You can read the story of the **Good Samaritan** in the Bible in Luke 10:25–37.

DAY FOUR: **Jackie Robinson** was the first African American major-league baseball player. **Martin Luther King Jr.** was a civil-rights leader in the 1950s and '60s, who was killed because of his efforts to win the right for all people to be treated equally, no matter their race or skin color. **Helen Keller** was both deaf and blind, but in spite of these challenges, she became an author, speaker, and political activist.

DAY FIVE: **Communism** is a political movement in which all property is meant to be owned collectively rather than by individuals. The centralized government becomes the ultimate power and is often oppressive to the people it oversees. Religion is generally discouraged, restricted, and in many cases, persecuted.

DAY SIX: On **September 11, 2001** (sometimes called 9/11), several airplanes were hijacked by terrorists, who crashed two of the planes into the two World Trade Center towers in New York City, and another into the Pentagon (the United States military headquarters) in Washington DC. Heroic passengers forced the fourth plane to crash in a Pennsylvania field to keep it from reaching its target. Nearly three thousand people were killed that day.

A **plastic surgeon** is a doctor who helps people by reconstructing parts of their bodies that may have been deformed through an accident or injury. A **pediatrician** is a doctor who specializes in treating children.

Muslims follow Islam, a religion based on the teachings of the prophet Muhammad. Muslims call their god "Allah." Christians believe that Muhammad was a false prophet.

notes

Day 1

1. Ace Collins, *Stories Behind Women of Extraordinary Faith* (Grand Rapids: Zondervan, 2008), 189–90.
2. Ibid., 189.

Day 2

1. Ron Hall and Denver Moore with Lynn Vincent, *Same Kind of Different as Me* (Nashville: Thomas Nelson, 2006), 3.
2. Ibid., 3–4.
3. Hall, *Same Kind of Different*, quoted in Ron Hall, "Who Is Your Neighbor," Life Today, LIFE Outreach International, www.lifetoday.org/site/News2?page=NewsArticle&id=6879&security=1&news_iv_ctrl=1061 (accessed August 27, 2010).
4. Ibid.
5. Hall, *Same Kind of Different*, 4.

Day 3

1. Gilbert V. Beers, "A Theology to Die By," *Christianity Today* (February 6, 1987): 11, quoted in Dennis Rainey with David Boehi, *The Tribute: What Every Parent Longs to Hear* (Nashville: Thomas Nelson, 1994), 59–61.
2. Gene Fedele, *Heroes of the Faith* (Gainesville, FL: Bridge-Logos, 2003), 228–29.

Day 4

1. Mrs. Howard Taylor, *Borden of Yale* (Minneapolis: Bethany House, 1988), 53.

2. Ibid., 153.
3. Eileen Scott, "'No Reserve,' 'No Retreat,' 'No Regrets,'" *Ivy League Christian Observer* (Fall 2009), involve.christian-union.org/site/News2?page+NewsArticle&id+7569 (accessed 8/31/10).
4. Ibid.
5. Taylor, 7.
6. Ibid., 187.
7. Scott.

Day 5

1. Dialogue quoted from dcTalk and the Voice of the Martyrs, *Jesus Freaks: Stories of Those Who Stood for Jesus* (Tulsa, OK: Albury Publishing, 1999), 63.
2. Ibid., 64.

Day 6

1. Susan Olasky, "Full Compassion," *World*, May 31, 2008, www.worldmag.com/articles/14071 (accessed August 27, 2010).
2. Paul Lim, e-mail to the author, February 9, 2010.

Day 7

1. Brother Andrew with John and Elizabeth Sherrill, *God's Smuggler* (Grand Rapids: Chosen Books, 2001), 107.
2. Ibid., 107–108.
3. Ibid., 138–39.
4. Ibid., 165.
5. Ibid., 165–66.

photo credits

FRONT COVER

World Health—©Norman Pogson | Dreamstime.com

Hans Scholl, Sophie Scholl, and Christoph Probst—1942, used by permission of akg-images, London

Food bowl—©Sergey Goruppa | Dreamstime.com

William Borden—courtesy of the Archives of the Billy Graham Center, Wheaton, Illinois

PAGE VI

©iStockphoto.com (Floriana Barbu)

PAGE 2

WWII airplane—©Ivan Cholakov | Dreamstime.com

Hans Scholl, Sophie Scholl, and Christoph Probst—1942, used by permission of akg-images, London

Postage stamp—commons.wikimedia.org/wiki/File:DBP_1964_431_Hitlerattentat_Sophie_Scholl.jpg

Barbed wire—©iStockphoto.com (Steve Christensen)

PAGE 4

White rose—©iStockphoto.com (Jodie Coston)

PAGE 6

Denver Moore—courtesy of Same Kind of Different as Me, Dallas, TX

Homeless man—©Andrew Kazmierski | Dreamstime.com

Food bowl—©Sergey Goruppa | Dreamstime.com

Debbie Hall—courtesy of Same Kind of Different as Me, Dallas, TX

PAGE 8

Soup kitchen—©Bob Denelzen | Dreamstime.com

PAGE 10

Burning logs—©iStockphoto.com (Jon Naustdalslid)

Antique map—upload.wikimedia.org/wikipedia/commons/2/21/Blaeu_-_Nova_Belgica_et_Anglia_Nova_%28Detail_Hudson_Area%29.png

India map—©Marcio Silva | Dreamstime.com

Amy Carmichael—commons.wikimedia.org/wikieFile:Amy_Carmichael_with_children2.jpg

PAGE 12

Hymnal—©iStockphoto.com (wolv)

PAGE 14

William Borden—courtesy of the Archives of the Billy Graham Center, Wheaton, Illinois

Egypt—©Daniel Wiedemann | Dreamstime.com

Borden residence—photographed by Chicago Daily News, DN-0004590, used by permission, Chicago Historical Society

Bible—photos.com/Jupiter Images

PAGE 16

Hurdle racers—©iStockphoto.com (technotr)

PAGE 18

Richard and Sabina Wurmbrand—Used with permission of Voice of the Martyrs (www.persecution.com)

Barbed wire—©iStockphoto.com (Hal Bergman)

Globe—©bigstockphoto.com (Elena Elisseeva)

Prisoner—Good Salt Images (Jeff Preston)

PAGE 20

Flag—©Bruno1998 | Dreamstime.com

PAGE 22

Paul Lim—courtesy of Paul Lim

Ethiopia map—©Olira | Dreamstime.com

Woman with child—©Millaus | Dreamstime.com

World Health—©Norman Pogson Dreamstime.com

PAGE 24

Stethoscope—©iStockphoto.com (Neustockimages)

PAGE 26

Brother Andrew—courtesy of Open Doors, USA

Halt—©iStockphoto.com (eyejoy)

Volkswagen—©bigstockphoto.com (Luis Seco)

Policeman—©iStockphoto.com (jonya)

PAGE 28

Suitcase—©iStockphoto.com (claylib)

PAGE 37

Barbara Rainey—J. E. Stover Photography, Inc.

BACK COVER

Hurdlers—©iStockphoto.com (technotr)

Halt—©iStockphoto.com (eyejoy)

Brother Andrew—courtesy of Open Doors, USA

Barbed wire—©iStockphoto.com (Hal Bergman)

A LETTER FROM THE AUTHOR

Dear Reader,

My husband and I had six children in ten years. The wide range of their ages and personalities made leading our children in any kind of home-centered spiritual direction a daunting task. So when a parent asks me how to encourage a fifteen-year-old in his faith while not ignoring the childlike questions of his five-year-old sister, I understand the predicament.

Where can a parent find stories and learning activities that are relevant to all ages? That was my dilemma; I could find no resources for a family like mine. I found lots of stories and songs for preschoolers and devotionals for teens, but nothing that would appeal to all of my children *together*.

What I did discover was that the best and easiest vehicle for transferring truth to my children was through stories. Whatever success we might have achieved in spiritually training our family came through shared stories of faith and discussions with our kids about taking God's truth with them into their lives. From that experience was born my dream to create resources to help moms and dads who want to be instrumental in raising children who are Christ followers.

Parents need something that works, something that is easy, something that requires no preparation. These seven stories make that possible. And unlike most devotional books that feature different themes with each day's reading, this resource focuses on one character quality that all parents want to develop in their children—courage. By reinforcing this one topic, my hope is that you and your family will grow in understanding what courage looks like and how to be courageous for what is right.

Thanks for using this short family devotional. I pray that you and your children will grow together as you're inspired by the great faith of these men and women whose stories I've shared.

Barbara Rainey

Barbara Rainey is the mother of six adult children and the "Mimi" of sixteen grandchildren. She and her husband, Dennis, give leadership to FamilyLife, a ministry committed to helping marriages and families survive and thrive in our generation. Barbara has written several books, including *Thanksgiving: A Time to Remember, Barbara and Susan's Guide to the Empty Nest,* and *When Christmas Came.* The Raineys live in Little Rock, Arkansas.

You can read more from Barbara online at FamilyLifeMomblog.com.

ABOUT THE SERIES

With captivating true stories to read as a family, these seven-day
interactive devotionals from speaker and best-selling author Barbara
Rainey saturate minds and hearts with memorable accounts and
vivid illustrations of true heroes who made noble choices.

Each day also includes:

- A key Bible verse

- Questions to discuss together

- A suggested prayer

- A personal record of your family's
  character as it relates to these stories

Encounter real-life heroes right in your living room—
and begin to grow together in character as a family.